DATE DUE

Ancient and modern images of Sappho